Waiting in Joyful Hope

*Daily Reflections for
Advent and Christmas
2021–2022*

Catherine Upchurch

LITURGICAL PRESS
Collegeville, Minnesota

www.litpress.org

Nihil Obstat: Rev. Robert Harren, J.C.L., *Censor Deputatus.*
Imprimatur: ✠ Most Rev. Donald J. Kettler, J.C.L., D.D., Bishop of
St. Cloud, January 21, 2021.

Cover design by Monica Bokinskie. Cover art courtesy of Getty
Images.

ISSN: 1550-803X
ISBN: 978-0-8146-6561-9   978-0-8146-6586-2 (ebook)

Introduction

When I started this project, I had a confident sense of my understanding of the Advent and Christmas seasons. I still do. But I have to say that engaging with the texts of Scripture so directly for each day has renewed my conviction that we can always expect God to be about making things new. Having gotten used to the cadence of the readings each year of my life is comforting, but what is wonderful is how I will inevitably hear something new or previously unnoticed in the familiar readings. It's like being given fresh ears or new hearing aids!

The Scriptures, of course, do not change; our lives, however, do change. We bring ourselves to the Bible's stories and teachings—our life circumstances make us curious in new ways, our learnings and leanings evolve over time, and our once firm set of expectations fade away. It is in this dialogue between sacred texts and our life experiences that we discover God still at work in us and in our world. We find that familiar passages take on layers of meaning when we allow God to speak through them with study and prayer.

As I completed this collection of reflections on the daily readings for the Advent and Christmas seasons, for some reason I thought of a simple necklace of mine that is made of mabe pearls. These pearls are not the typically round ones, but have a flat wavy appearance. They come in lustrous shades of silvery white, pinks, blues, and greens. The first time my necklace broke, I lost a few of the pearls but strung it back together. By the third time (obviously it is well worn), I realized I needed to knot between each bead to ensure I wouldn't lose any more of them shimmying across a floor. Each day of readings struck me as one of those pearls, each one with its own particular odd shape calling attention to itself while at the same time wanting to be part of the whole.

Advent is a time to anticipate the whole. It brings together centuries of expectation and longing and invites us to imagine the world anew, to pick up the beads of tradition and see how beautifully they fit together in a new and fresh arrangement. The Christmas season wraps up this freshness and presents it as a gift to a world in need of beauty. Just as great artists agonize over the pieces they create and often live in poverty while creating a body of work, the beauty that God offers us in these seasons may ask something of us—releasing some preconceived ideas, spending time and energy, and some soul searching.

The Advent and Christmas seasons are filled already with obligations and activities, some of them connected with our parish communities, and you may wonder how in the world you will fit in one more thing. But, just maybe, you and I can make our few minutes with the readings each day not "one more thing" but the best thing.

FIRST WEEK OF ADVENT

November 28: First Sunday of Advent

Shake Off the Drowsiness

Readings: Jer 33:14-16; 1 Thess 3:12–4:2; Luke 21:25-28, 34-36

Scripture:
"Beware that your hearts do not become drowsy. . . ."
  (Luke 21:34)

Reflection: When traveling with my brother and his family some years ago, we stopped in a local grocery store known for its back-room diner and piles of fish served family style. The evening we sat down there at a simple table, we were happily exhausted after a day in the sun, and when the plates of food arrived we dug in. It wasn't long before my young nephew's head was bobbing as he fought off sleep. He'd catch himself and sit up straight, and then in no time at all he'd be bobbing drowsily again. His heavy eyelids were our signal to get the kids to bed. We adults weren't far behind. This kind of drowsiness is the kind we long for, knowing we'll have a good night's sleep ahead.

The drowsiness that Jesus warns against is the kind that allows us to shut our eyes, not from weariness, but out of willful ignorance, or laziness, or even selfishness. We wish we could avoid the difficult situations in our lives. We hope we will not have to do the hard work of righting a wrong. We want to turn off the news and ignore the plight of others whose needs make us uncomfortable. These anxieties of

6   *First Week of Advent*

daily life can have a numbing effect on us. Jesus knew this well, and he shook his disciples awake. He shook them with his words, his encounters, and his critique of the world in which he and his disciples found themselves. He shakes us awake too, urging us to be alert to what is happening in and around us.

Meditation: As we begin this season of expectation, we are awakened to a different rhythm. We become aware once again that it is not enough merely to go through the motions of daily life. In these weeks, we allow our hearts and minds to be attuned to God-in-the-world—in the past, in the present, and in the future. Advent reminds us that God is already at work. Does this truth quicken our hearts and shape our relationships with the world?

Prayer: Jesus, rouse us from our drowsiness. Help us sit upright, listen for your voice, and watch for your presence. Create in us the desire and the will to enter into each day of this season anticipating how we will be asked to help others know your saving presence.

November 29: Monday of the First Week of Advent

Take Instruction

Readings: Isa 2:1-5; Matt 8:5-11

Scripture:
"Come, let us climb the LORD's mountain . . .
That he may instruct us in his ways,
   and we may walk in his paths." (Isa 2:3)

Reflection: Our best teachers continue to have a place in our hearts. We look up to them, for their wisdom and their kindness, for their honor and their strength. How fitting that "looking up" to others is the way we express admiration for those we wish to imitate—a strict teacher we discover showing compassion for a struggling student, a demanding mentor who draws from us gifts we did not know we had, or a parent whose discipline is wise and forward thinking. In his own way, the prophet Isaiah invites God's people to look up to the best instructor of all. They are to ascend the hills of Jerusalem to the house of God, the temple. The instruction they receive will get them in shape to walk in the ways of God.

We also are being asked to get in shape, to open our ears and our hearts, and to figuratively strap on our shoes so that we are ready to walk in God's way. Today's passage from Isaiah gives us a key to God's instruction. Speaking for God, Isaiah describes a world where swords will no longer be needed and nations will no longer train for war. The Second

Vatican Council takes up this call, saying, "People of the present generation should realize that they will have to render an account of their warlike behavior." While this may sound naïve, it is nonetheless the vision that is ahead of us as we learn to walk the path God lays out for us.

Meditation: How ardently do we hope to be instructed in God's ways? Do we create opportunities through Bible study and prayer? Through friendships with others who also love God? Through spiritual reading that is uplifting and challenging? Consider this day how such instruction has informed your life, not just as a child but as an adult, with adult concerns and responsibilities. On this Advent day, will you ascend God's mountain in your own heart and find God ready to speak with you? Will you be ready to listen, even if God's words are difficult to digest?

Prayer: Equip us, O God, with minds and hearts ready to imagine a world where plowshares are more necessary than weapons, and food more plentiful than swords. Strengthen our resolve to learn your ways and recognize your path. Give us the grace to stay the course.

November 30: Saint Andrew, Apostle

Welcome the Good News

Readings: Rom 10:9-18; Matt 4:18-22

Scripture:
How beautiful are the feet of those who bring the good news!
  (Rom 10:15)

Reflection: Just after the Second Vatican Council, Catholic adults were hungering for a way to enter into the Bible and its rich gifts for us. Encouraged by the work of the council, a group in Arkansas enlisted the help of a local Benedictine priest who had recently completed his academic work in the area of Scripture. It was a time of awakening in the church, and adults wanted the opportunity to learn the Bible, grow in their faith, and fall more deeply in love with Jesus. Twenty-five years later, at a celebration for this Bible study ministry, one of the participants raised a toast with these words, "To Father Jerome and his beautiful feet!" Indeed, he helped to bring the Good News of Jesus to life in our midst.

In today's first reading from Romans, Paul reminds his readers (ancient and current) that the gift of faith comes from what is heard. Of course he is encouraging the followers of Jesus to get our feet going and bring the Good News to others, but he is also encouraging all to welcome the Good News. Paul invites us to experience the beauty of God's word, and we do this every time we prepare ourselves to hear the daily readings, each time we ponder a passage until it speaks to us, and most especially when we invite the Lord to inhabit our minds and hearts. How else will we come to recognize the coming of Christ?

Meditation: Consider whose feet are beautiful in your life because they have delivered God's word to you—a pastor, a parent, a spouse, a friend, a teacher, a writer or speaker. While we must come to Christ personally, we rarely do so on our own. Someone has shared the Good News with us and invited us to respond. In this time of expectant waiting, we have the opportunity to gratefully recognize these ambassadors of the Good News in our personal lives.

Prayer: O God, who chooses to use our feet for your purposes, send us where you will. May our comings and goings in the lives of others bring goodness into their lives. And may those who come our way announcing your presence find a welcome home with us. Bless those who teach, those who preach, and those whose works reveal your goodness.

December 1: Wednesday of the First Week of Advent

Stretch Your Imagination

Readings: Isa 25:6-10a; Matt 15:29-37

Scripture:
"Where could we ever get enough bread in this deserted
   place to satisfy such a crowd?" (Matt 15:33)

Reflection: Deserted places are the backdrop for many a film.
Old westerns used to bring the viewer into a scene where
the buildings are all weathered, the tumbleweed is blowing
through town, and the saloon door creeks on what is left of
its rusty hinges. It is desolate; it is a blank slate for trouble,
and we, the viewers, are all set to see what unfolds.

Deserted places are also the setting for many scenes
throughout Scripture. But in our sacred texts these places
provide the opportunity for encounter and conversion—the
freed slaves come to know the God of liberation in the Sinai
Desert, the prophet Elijah encounters God in the tiny whispering sounds of his desert cave, Jesus defeats Satan's temp-
tations in the Judean Desert, and John the Baptist uses a
meager source of water in the desert to baptize those who
repent.

Today's gospel finds Jesus surrounded by massive crowds
for a three-day marathon of teaching. It is a spontaneous
gathering on a hillside, near the Sea of Galilee and away
from familiar villages and homes. Jesus knows he cannot

send the people away hungry, and when he mentions this to his disciples, they see only a deserted place. No kitchen, no fire pit, no food. They have no imagination about the power of Jesus to transform a deserted place into a picnic! They are just beginning to realize that Jesus is about abundance, not scarcity. Meager provisions are not an obstacle but a divine opportunity.

Meditation: We know deserted places, both within and around us. The challenge for us is to recognize that these are the places where God waits to meet us. They are not blank movie sets waiting for trouble to blow in like a tumbleweed; these deserted places are where God will nurture us with the solid food of sound teaching. We are being asked to approach these places that feel empty and desolate with an expectation of encountering the God of abundance, the God who will take what we offer and make it bountiful.

Prayer: You, O God of desolate places, come to meet us. Shape our vision so that we see abundance instead of scarcity, and ability instead of inadequacy. Set our eyes and our hearts on what we can offer rather than what we lack. Multiply the little gifts that we have so that, with your grace, they become sufficient.

December 2: Thursday of the First Week of Advent

Build on Rock

Readings: Isa 26:1-6; Matt 7:21, 24-27

Scripture:
"Everyone who listens to these words of mine and acts
on them will be like a wise man who built his house on
rock." (Matt 7:24)

Reflection: The Middle East consists of various sizes of rock—
from majestic rock mountains, to smooth boulder plateaus,
to the tiniest grain of sand. It takes centuries for a rock the
size of one's hand to be reduced to sand, and the process is
a complex melding of water, sunlight, and friction. When
Jesus talks about building a house on rock, he is working
with the reality he knows as a son of a hardened landscape.
Rock provides the stable foundation that will last over time,
in fact, over generations. A house built on sand, the tiniest
remains of rock, will soon wash away.

Isaiah, in today's first reading, proclaims that "the Lord
is an eternal Rock." This metaphor for God is also popular
throughout the psalms. Since Jesus and his listeners are
schooled in the psalms and prophets of their tradition, he is
telling his followers that a rock foundation is important not
just when building a house, but when building a life. It is
not enough to simply lay out the plans for our lives, as
thoughtful as they may be; to ensure our plans are solid, we

are called to share our plans with the master builder and listen for a response. We stay in dialogue with the builder to make adjustments that are needed, even to start again if necessary. Building a full and sturdy life, exposed as we are to all kinds of elements, demands a strong foundation.

Meditation: We live in a world that exposes us to numerous interests competing for our attention. Many of these, to reference Paul's letter to the Philippians (4:8), are true, honorable, just, pure, lovely, and gracious. In some of the world's interests we discover God's very presence. But the priorities of our world and our culture are often at odds with the Good News. Determining what is rock solid and will endure, and what is more like sand that will be washed away, requires our careful attention and prayerful discernment. Advent offers us a time that is well suited to such self-examination.

Prayer: This Advent, O Lord, we invite you to look over the plans we have for our lives. Help us to build a solid foundation for our big dreams, a foundation built on your very presence and permeated with your wisdom. We want our lives to reflect your values and priorities, and our homes to welcome those searching for the firm foundation you provide.

December 3: Saint Francis Xavier, Priest

Embrace Joy

Readings: Isa 29:17-24; Matt 9:27-31

Scripture:
The lowly will ever find joy in the LORD. . . .
For the tyrant will be no more. . . . (Isa 29:19, 20)

Reflection: So often I hear parents, and aunts and uncles, and grandparents saying something along the lines of, "I just want my children to be happy." While the sentiment is understandable (Who wants their son or daughter to be sad? Or an adult child to be morose?), surely what we want for our children is more than happiness. Happiness is fleeting and usually a response to outside circumstances such as a great party, a promotion, or an athletic victory. While these things can make us feel happy, the feeling does not last; it simply can't because circumstances change. Joy, on the other hand, especially finding joy in the Lord, is not about feelings. It is rooted in the conviction that God is with us through whatever circumstances in which we find ourselves, and that our lives have purpose because of God's presence with us and in us. That conviction is perhaps closer to what we truly want for our children and for ourselves.

The prophet Isaiah assures the lowly that joy will return as tyrants fall. At the time of Isaiah, Judah was in the midst of crumbling from internal corruption and external political and military pressure. The prophet's call was to remind God's people of their identity and of God's powerful presence with them. The question for us is whether we acknowledge our own lowliness and befriend it, or whether we are on the side of tyrants who cannot allow themselves to be vulnerable enough to rely on God's mercy.

Meditation: The French priest and philosopher Teilhard de Chardin is credited with saying that joy is the most infallible sign of the presence of God. And while joy is listed by Paul as a fruit of the Spirit (Gal 5:22), many Christians appear to be awfully glum. How we carry God's presence in us affects our dispositions, our relationships, our acts of service, and our progress as disciples. If we're missing the joy, this season provides us the opportunity to remember whose we are. By renewing our identity, we may just tap into that deep well of joy.

Prayer: Stir within us, O God, a profound sense of your abiding presence. Even in Advent as we look forward to celebrating the birth of your son in Bethlehem, we also anticipate your coming again. Let this next coming be a source of joy for us, and not dread, as we work to dismantle what tyrants have built, and as we discover our continuing desire for your mercy and love.

December 4: Saturday of the First Week of Advent

Give without Cost

Readings: Isa 30:19-21, 23-26; Matt 9:35–10:1, 5a, 6-8

Scripture:
"Without cost you have received; without cost you are to
  give." (Matt 10:8)

Reflection: If Christmas is the season of giving, then Advent
may well be the season of list making and gift buying. At
least, that is the norm in our culture, driven as we are to plan
for a perfect celebration with family or friends, for the perfect
choir selections for Christmas Mass, and for the perfect meal
to share with others. We agonize over the gifts we will pur-
chase and how they will be wrapped. But being "all wrapped
up" in these rituals of December might just prevent us from
finding joy in the imperfect and discovering the best gifts
we want to share with others.

When Jesus commissions his closest followers in today's
gospel, he reminds them that their ministry is a continuation
of his. They will cure the sick, raise the dead, cleanse lepers,
and drive out demons. We, too, share that ministry. We are
commissioned to offer the healing touch of Jesus to those in
our lives who are physically ill or mentally spent. We have
the opportunity to help others identify what has died in them
so that it can be resurrected with God's help. We can provide
a bridge of acceptance to those who feel excluded from com-

munity. And we can proclaim the truth that good will always triumph over evil. These gifts are the priceless treasures we have been given. They are the same gifts that we can share without cost in this season. We will still wrap our presents and joyfully give them, but the ones that will last will not need to be wrapped.

Meditation: Perhaps what we want most, and what we hope to share, is a deep experience of God. It's not magical; it cannot be purchased; it will not tarnish with age. It is freely given by the very God who made each of us, as well as the heavens and the earth. This gift does require something from us—attentiveness. How will we train our hearts to recognize God's desire to give us what we most need? How will we share what our hearts receive unless we look for the openings, the opportunities to continue what is begun as Christ takes up residence in us?

Prayer: Giver of all good gifts, we turn to you with gratitude. Thank you for knowing what we need most, and giving it freely to us. Keeper of hearts, stand at attention with us as we look for opportunities to share what we have received.

SECOND WEEK OF ADVENT

December 5: Second Sunday of Advent

Clear the Way for God to Enter

Readings: Bar 5:1-9; Phil 1:4-6, 8-11; Luke 3:1-6

Scripture:
"The winding roads shall be made straight,
and the rough ways made smooth. . . ." (Luke 3:5)

Reflection: For many years my youngest brother enjoyed mainly road cycling, but in recent years mountain biking has become his preference. The rocks and roots challenge his skills and endurance, and the out-of-the-way paths provide the best scenery. At the end of these rides he feels a deep sense of reward and pleasure. All I can see, however, is rough terrain, and I can well imagine the aching muscles from all that high-impact riding. I think the idea of making rough ways smooth, as Luke quotes the prophet Isaiah, sounds mighty fine in comparison. Of course, Luke was not talking about cycling, but there are some valuable lessons from that discipline that might apply.

The coming of Jesus did not, and has not, made all the rough roads smooth or the winding ways straight. Most of us will admit that our journey with the Lord has been quite winding, and sometimes bumpy, even jarring. With the benefit of reflection, we might also acknowledge that these twists and turns test our endurance and sharpen our senses to find that God is present. That kind of triumph in the midst of hardship is indeed satisfying. We might even be willing to admit that beauty is extra sweet when coming out of those curves and overcoming obstacles. Could our continued journeys over these tough terrains be part of what smooths them out? Could it be that God is using us to make a way for his son's next coming?

Meditation: In today's gospel reading, John the Baptist repeats the ancient words of Isaiah to offer comfort. John assures those coming to him for the baptism of repentance that God's work of redemption is continual. But it's not only about offering comfort. The passage begins, *"Prepare the way of the LORD."* Their cooperation with God is essential. The same is true for us. This season reminds us that the work of spiritual preparation is ongoing. As we make our way back and forth over the rocks and stones of bad habits and attitudes, the way becomes smoother and we realize we are clearing a way for God to enter.

Prayer: Your people have always yearned to welcome you into their hearts, O Lord. We join the ranks of those whose desire to welcome you is matched by a determination to clear a path where you may enter more freely. Come, Lord Jesus.

Strengthen Others

Readings: Isa 35:1-10; Luke 5:17-26

Scripture:
Say to those whose hearts are frightened:
   Be strong, fear not! (Isa 35:4)

Reflection: One of my favorite psalms proclaims, "You shall not fear the terror of the night" (Ps 91:5). I called that to mind the first time a loud noise in my home awakened me in the middle of the night. To be honest, the words of the psalm were of no comfort as long as I did not know the source of that noise. In fact, it seems to me that a few ounces of caution, maybe even a healthy sense of fear, are needed in some circumstances. Fear can be the instinct that protects us from dangers we can avoid.

I feel certain that the psalmist is speaking mainly of other terrors of the night, those that rob us of our peace and our sense of purpose, those that freeze us emotionally or spiritually. The Bible is peppered with close to four hundred reminders to fear not. Surely that tells us that fear is so natural it must be addressed, but it also tells us that fear is not meant to shape our core identity.

When Isaiah says, "Be strong, fear not!" he is addressing God's people captured and taken into exile in Babylon. All around them is foreign. The familiar reminders of God's presence—the temple and its courts, the royal palace—have been destroyed. Of course they are fearful. But God does not want fear to define them. He sends the prophet Isaiah to encourage them, literally to fill them with courage in the darkest of days and nights. When our hearts are fearful, we turn to God to give us courage.

Meditation: Who are the fearful of heart in our midst? The worker who lost her job, the child raised in a home with abuse, the athlete whose career is cut short, the woman whose pregnancy comes without a safety net, the elderly neighbor who lives on a fixed income? We can be the ones who provide God's strength and walk with others through their fear. Advent reminds us that God sent Jesus to walk with us, to be the source of strength and courage.

Prayer: Jesus, when fear wants to leave us cowering, we stand tall knowing you walk with us. When fear threatens to paralyze our efforts, you call us forward. Remind us that in your coming among us, we have a strong and faithful companion even through the darkest night.

Reconsider Your Image of God

Readings: Isa 40:1-11; Matt 18:12-14

Scripture:
"[I]t is not the will of your heavenly Father that one of these little ones be lost." (Matt 18:14)

Reflection: When I was growing up, I had the distinct impression that very few would enter the gates of heaven, be those gates pearly or otherwise! The path is narrow; it is harder for a camel to get through the eye of a needle; we can be caught off guard on the day of the Lord. It simply seemed impossible except for those who led exemplary lives, or died as martyrs.

I was failing to see and hear that while God prepares us for hardship, it is not God's *will* to lose any of us. God's desire is that all shall experience the fullness of life. Our gospel today assures us that God is like the shepherd who seeks out the lost. In another gospel passage, Jesus tells his followers, "Do not be afraid . . . for your Father is *pleased* to give you the kingdom" (Luke 12:32; emphasis added). Saint Paul was so deeply convicted of this that he wrote to the Ephesians, "[God] destined us for adoption to himself through Jesus Christ" (Eph 1:5), and to Timothy that God "wills everyone to be saved" (1 Tim 2:4).

This divine desire for our salvation does not let us off the hook to behave however we wish. Rather, it calls forth from us our true selves, that self that is rooted in the image of God in which we are made. And when we stumble along the way, or stray from our deepest identity as God's adopted sons and daughters, God does not give up on us.

Meditation: In our culture, we tend to give a high priority to being law abiding. Perhaps this is because we know obedience to the law generally sets out parameters for harmony and creates a sense of order in a community. From a Christian viewpoint, however, being law abiding is not a guarantee of spiritual reward. We are called to a higher form of harmony, one that flows from an ongoing and always deepening relationship with the God who loves us first, best, and always, and with our neighbor who also is worthy of being loved in this way.

Prayer: O God, shepherd of a rather unruly flock, teach us to listen for your voice. Help us to allow your love to penetrate our consciousness. Seek us out when we stray, gather us in your arms, and return us to the flock you tend.

December 8:
The Immaculate Conception of the Blessed Virgin Mary

Allow Your Heart to Ponder

Readings: Gen 3:9-15, 20; Eph 1:3-6, 11-12; Luke 1:26-38

Scripture:
"Hail, full of grace! The Lord is with you." But she was
greatly troubled . . . and pondered. . . . (Luke 1:28, 29)

Reflection: "The Lord is with you." Those words sound comforting all these centuries later because we know the out-
come. Mary, however, was greatly troubled in that moment.
Who wouldn't be troubled by such a direct encounter with
God's messenger? Especially a messenger associated, up to
this point in Jewish tradition, with the end times (Dan 8:15-
27)? Mary's initial response, with that history in mind,
sounds quite understandable. The gospel passage uses a
particular word, "ponder," to describe what Mary did next.
A similar word is used to describe Mary's response to the
shepherds who visited her newborn child and said that an
angel had revealed he was Messiah and Lord (Luke 2:19).
　　Pondering is often described as a mental activity. It can
mean that a person weighs the value of something by giving
it serious consideration. Another definition that gives attention to the heart is perhaps better. In Semitic languages, such
as Hebrew and Aramaic, the heart is the center of the person,
the place where reason, emotion, imagination, conscience,

and prayer abide together. To ponder is to contemplate, to chew on something while trying to make sense of it, to allow the heart to interact with it as it determines whether to surrender. This is the kind of pondering Mary surely did in her encounter with the angel Gabriel. It was only after she pondered that she could summon the courage to listen to more, to ask how God's work in her would happen, and to joyfully respond, "Yes!" Mary's pondering surely lasted her entire life and required many surrenders of her heart.

Meditation: The words of the Hail Mary, based on today's gospel scene, were taught to many of us as children, and we have repeated them thousands of times. We can become so familiar with Scripture's words and images that we miss their ability to slice through the routine rhythms of life. Or we can allow those same words and images to heighten our awareness of how God moves in the world—in this case how God worked in the life of one woman, and how God works in us. What is God asking you to ponder today?

Prayer: In these Advent days, we call to mind that the Blessed Mother was once a simple girl who chose to listen to God's messenger, a girl who took the time to ponder. Help us, O God, to slow down long enough to hear your voice, and quietly enough to ponder your words.

Read from a Position without Power

Readings: Isa 41:13-20; Matt 11:11-15

Scripture:
"[A]mong those born of women there has been none
greater than John the Baptist; yet the least in the
Kingdom of heaven is greater than he." (Matt 11:11)

Reflection: Sometimes before I actually sit through a full-length film, I have seen the trailer, a two-to-three-minute highlight reel that either spoils the entire plot or piques my interest enough to watch for its release date. Today's gospel account feels like one of those trailers. The narrator is the main character of the story, Jesus, and it features an early costar, John the Baptist. The context is misunderstanding, and even threats, against the two great figures who usher in the reign of God. Far from spoiling the plot, this trailer has me hooked and I want to know more.

Both men have upset the status quo—John by preparing a way for Jesus and calling for repentance, and Jesus by coming among them without all the trappings of what many in power would have been more comfortable with. By this point in the story, John has already been put in prison and soon will be executed, and Jesus is proclaiming a kingdom where the normal roles for the haves and the have-nots are reversed. In fact, in the kingdom where God reigns, it is the least who are the greatest. Jesus illustrates this time and time again in his words and deeds throughout his public ministry, creating greater tension with those in power and greater hope in the lives of those on the fringes of society. When we read the Bible, it matters whether we are reading from the viewpoint of power or from a position without power.

Meditation: When we read the Bible, we necessarily hear its meaning from within our cultural context and our position in society. But we cannot stop there if we want to uncover deeper layers of meaning. In Jesus' time, those without access to power (religious or political) were largely ignored, but the message of Jesus put these powerless populations front and center. He challenged the people of his time who wielded power to listen from a different perspective. Our challenge, too, is to put ourselves in the position of those who are "the least" and determine whether we will allow Jesus' words to liberate us from norms that conflict with the gospel.

Prayer: Jesus, teach us to open our minds and hearts to the power of your message. Remind us to read and pray with your teachings from the perspective of the poor, the forgotten, the imprisoned, and the outcast. Prepare us to greet you with poverty of spirit.

Lament and Learn

Readings: Isa 48:17-19; Matt 11:16-19

Scripture:
If you would hearken to my commandments,
   your prosperity would be like a river,
   and your vindication like the waves of the sea. . . .
      (Isa 48:18)

Reflection: I'm sometimes tempted to revisit the past, particularly past mistakes or pain. *If only I hadn't . . .*, I think to myself; *If only they hadn't . . .* These are wistful wishes to undo what has been done by me or to me, to imagine how things might have been different. I have discovered that this type of ruminating changes nothing. It is far better to lament and learn, which is precisely what is happening in our reading today from Isaiah. God laments that the people of Judah have ignored the life-giving commands of the covenant and instead put themselves in the position to be held in captivity in Babylon. God is inviting his people to enter into lament with him so that they can truly learn how to live.

God's lament isn't a morbid dwelling on Judah's past sins, though God definitely uses Isaiah to help them see their sin: the idolatry of worshiping false gods and entering into foreign alliances, as well as a lack of mercy and justice for the poor in their midst. God's lament is more the cry of a parent who wants their young adult child to learn from the past and move forward with more maturity. Such lament acknowledges sin for what it is and then provides images that paint a picture of what can be: peace like a river, vindication like the constant waves of the sea. Look around and see what images from nature might be calling the church today to turn to the Lord.

Meditation: Though repentance is not the primary focus of Advent, repentance is definitely part of how we prepare ourselves for the great coming of Christ. Lament is critical to that process. We identify the ways we and our world are out of step in our walk with the world, and we mourn. How could individual lament help redirect each of us? What might require lament from our faith community in these days as we prepare the way for the Lord?

Prayer: O God, we come before you with a sincere desire to walk in your ways. Help us to acknowledge our failings and to look for the signs of renewal in our lives. In the winter landscapes, help us to find images of peace that will turn our hearts to you.

December 11: Saturday of the Second Week of Advent

Seek God's Face

Readings: Sir 48:1-4, 9-11; Matt 17:9a, 10-13

Scripture:
Lord, make us turn to you; let us see your face and we
shall be saved. (Ps 80:4)

Reflection: When my youngest brother was a small guy, he
was weary of shopping with my mom and me in a local
department store. He asked if he could go to see the toys,
and after a good bit of instruction from my mom about stay-
ing right there and we would join him shortly, he set off. Two
minutes later, we went two aisles over and he was nowhere
to be found. He went to see the toys all right, but he had in
mind the toy store out in the mall. We were frantic, desperate
to find him. Now, of course, he didn't know he was lost, but
we sure did. I'll never forget my mom's face when she finally
laid eyes on him innocently playing with a race car. It's that
expression that I picture when I think of seeing God's face,
how joy-filled he is to see our faces upturned to his.

Today's responsorial psalm is nestled between two readings that reference the prophet Elijah. This is the prophet
who warned Israel and their king against worshiping false
gods, and successfully challenged the false prophets on
Mount Carmel. This is the prophet who fled to a cave for
safety, hoping to encounter God in thunder and lightning

but instead discovering God in a gentle whisper. This is the prophet who was taken up to heaven in a chariot and was believed to return before the end of time. This is the prophet who appears alongside Moses and Jesus at the transfiguration, symbolizing the fullness of time is upon us. Now is the time to turn our faces and see God there having found us.

Meditation: The season of Advent is brimming with centuries of longing—longing for the Messiah, longing for God's mercy, longing for God's light and goodness—ultimately, longing to see God's face and live. In Jesus, we do just that. We look upon the face of God in Christ, and we begin to see God's face in those we live with, those we work with, and those we meet throughout the ordinary events of our days. Ask for the grace to look upon the face of God.

Prayer: Jesus, the Christ, you are the face of God, gazing at us with love and mercy. Let us see your eyes in those who look to us for help, and your smile in those who cheer us. In tears and in laughter, we know you are near.

THIRD WEEK OF ADVENT

December 12: Third Sunday of Advent

Rejoice with Gladness

Readings: Zeph 3:14-18a; Phil 4:4-7; Luke 3:10-18

Scripture:
The LORD, your God, is in your midst,
  a mighty savior;
he will rejoice over you with gladness,
  and renew you in his love. . . . (Zeph 3:17)

Reflection: I remember being overwhelmed by a sense of joy years ago at a dear friend's wedding. The congregation reflected back to the couple what they were exuding from the moment guests began arriving. The bride didn't hide away so her groom could not see her; the groom wasn't off with his groomsmen nervously awaiting his entrance into the sanctuary. No, they were both at the doors of the church, hugging and kissing their guests, welcoming us into the ceremony and, more importantly, into their lives as a couple. We had no doubt that God was present as they vowed themselves to each other and invited us to bless their journey with our support.

God desires to rejoice over us in the same way that these two people rejoiced over each other and shared their gladness with us. Jesus is God's clear promise to renew his love over and over throughout history. Prophets such as Zephaniah and John the Baptist announced his coming, raising hopeful expectation. Paul proclaimed from a prison cell that, in Christ, God provides peace beyond understanding. Paul even exhorted those who corresponded with him to rejoice always. On this Gaudete Sunday (from the Latin word meaning "rejoice"), we acclaim that Jesus' coming among us centuries ago has spread ripples of God's joy throughout history.

My friends who married many moons ago in great joy have also experienced great sadness and deep challenges. But that original joy sustains them, much as the joy of that original season of expectation in Bethlehem has sustained the world.

Meditation: Immediately following the Lord's Prayer at Mass, the prayer of the priest contains these wonderful lines: "[T]hat by the help of your mercy, / we may be always free from sin / and safe from all distress, / as we await the blessed hope / and the coming of our Savior, Jesus Christ." There is a great difference between simply waiting and being expectant. One is a test of patience, the other is an expression of hope. Let us be people of blessed hope.

Prayer: O Lord, our God, your son's coming in Bethlehem was a cause of great joy on earth and in heaven. You placed the savior in our midst to renew your love in us and for us. As we await his second coming, free us from distress and fill us with blessed hope.

Say Yes to the Authority of Jesus

Readings: Num 24:2-7, 15-17a; Matt 21:23-27

Scripture:

"By what authority are you doing these things? And who
gave you this authority?" (Matt 21:23b)

Reflection: When I first became a teacher, I had a room full
of third grade students and I was teaching in the same classroom where I was once a student. I had a sense that at any
moment my former principal would enter the room and ask
what I thought I was doing taking over the classroom. Never
mind that she was still the principal and the one who hired
me. It was she who invested me with the authority I needed
to run the classroom and teach the children who would be
with me day after day. I felt inadequate initially, almost a
pretender. Over time, I grew in confidence and understood
that whatever authority I had was only valid when it served
the children in my care.

Authority is a tricky thing. It is the necessary companion
of responsibility. When abused and disconnected from responsibility, it becomes a dangerous weapon. Jesus was
questioned about his authority because he identified the
abuse of authority by some of the scribes and Pharisees. His
words and deeds reveal a deep commitment to his responsibility to announce and build the kingdom of God, and it

is clear that this heavenly kingdom challenged the religious and political kingdoms of his day. In today's gospel, Jesus is asked a legitimate question: Who gives you the authority to challenge us? His questioners, however, were not prepared to accept his word for it, and so Jesus continued to reveal through his ministry that his authority came from God.

Meditation: At the close of Matthew's gospel (28:16-20), the resurrected Jesus appears to his followers. Even while they are still somewhat doubtful about all that has transpired, he gives them authority to continue his mission. We take up this responsibility to evangelize as the constant mission of the church. Saint John Paul II wrote, "Missionary activity renews the church, revitalizes faith and Christian identity, and offers fresh enthusiasm and new incentive. Faith is strengthened when it is given to others!" How are we obedient to the authority of Jesus that sends us forth? How might we embrace this mission more fully?

Prayer: Jesus, you embraced your mission to redeem the world by sharing God's love, mercy, and justice. We pray to accept your authority in our lives. May our attempts to continue your mission advance the kingdom you announced and embodied.

December 14: Saint John of the Cross,
Priest and Doctor of the Church

Pay Attention to the Faithful Remnant

Readings: Zeph 3:1-2, 9-13; Matt 21:28-32

Scripture:
I will leave as a remnant in your midst
   a people humble and lowly,
Who shall take refuge in the name of the LORD. . . .
   (Zeph 3:12)

Reflection: My grandmother had an old black Singer sewing machine in the corner of her big kitchen. She saved bits and pieces of fabric from her projects so that she could sew small and stylish dresses, jackets, and pants for our dolls. I would marvel that she could neatly attach a little pocket or sew an armhole the size of my little finger. We loved hunting through her unused fabrics to find just the right remnant for her to use. She knew how to use something "left over," something that was small and insignificant, to make of it something new and fresh and sturdy.

In some ways that is what the prophet Zephaniah is talking about in today's reading. He's saying that in the midst of suffering, sin, and eventual exile, when it seems that faithfulness is gone and the covenant cannot be salvaged, God will find a way to make a people fresh and new. The notion of a faithful remnant is found throughout the writings of the prophets in particular. The prophets are charged by God to dismantle what is sinful and unjust in the societies of Judah and Israel, and then help those who repent and return to God to become a new creation. Those who were among the least in society, faithful but ignored, must have felt a distinct sense of having been cast aside, but God assures them that they are not forgotten: they are a faithful remnant who will see the promises of God fulfilled.

Meditation: Where do we look for the ways that God is using a faithful remnant in our parishes? In our families? In our personal lives? Are we humble enough to listen to the witness of others and to allow their experiences to touch our own? Are we humble enough to find in ourselves that glimmer of hope that God continues to act in us and in our world to bring about renewal?

Prayer: Being faithful often means being ready to repent and ready to hope again. In this Advent season, O God, use whatever remnants of faith you find among us to rebuild your people. Give us the humility to turn to you.

December 15: Wednesday of the Third Week of Advent

Look for the Evidence

Readings: Isa 45:6c-8, 18, 21c-25; Luke 7:18b-23

Scripture:
"Go and tell John what you have seen and heard: the blind
   regain their sight, the lame walk, lepers are cleansed, the
   deaf hear, the dead are raised, the poor have the good
   news proclaimed to them." (Luke 7:22)

Reflection: When Jesus was asked by John's disciples if he
was the one who was to come, the one they had been expect-
ing, a simple yes or no would not suffice. From the very start,
Jesus shapes his audience to move from curiosity to belief,
from observing to following. By telling John the Baptist's
disciples that they should simply lay out the evidence for
John, Jesus is telling them to engage in the process and do
the work that will be convincing. Allow the truth to rise to
the surface from the evidence presented.

Here in the midst of Advent we may wonder why the
church asks us to jump right into the interactions the adult
Jesus had with those surrounding him. Perhaps we are being
shaped to recognize that the child Jesus who will be born in
Bethlehem meets us throughout our lives as the adult Jesus
who unveils the radical way that God dwells with us. As
shocking as it is to anticipate the coming of God's son, his
taking on our very nature, how much more to acknowledge

that he comes to heal the sick, restore life, and honor the dignity of the poor. This is the evidence Jesus chooses to present as a testimony to his identity.

Meditation: Jesus seems to agree with the adage that actions speak louder than words. The gospels provide volumes of evidence that Jesus knows the importance of integrity, of speaking and acting from the very center of his identity. When he teaches about forgiving one's neighbor, he demonstrates it by forgiving his executioners. When he says that the eyes of the blind will be open and the deaf will hear, he publicly restores sight and hearing. When he talks about the fullness of life, he demonstrates it by raising his friend Lazarus and the son of a widow. He means what he says, and invests his life in living what he preaches. What evidence will be found in our lives to demonstrate that we are committed to Jesus?

Prayer: Jesus, your life gives witness to the very nature of God's love. Continue to shape us as your disciples so that our words and deeds will reveal our identity as your disciples.

Choose Peace

Readings: Isa 54:1-10; Luke 7:24-30

Scripture:
. . . My love shall never leave you
   nor my covenant of peace be shaken. . . . (Isa 54:10b)

Reflection: Today's first reading comes from a portion of Isaiah that addresses God's people in exile in Babylon. Their temple in Jerusalem has been destroyed by war, their capital city and surrounding towns are in ruins, and the land they received from God is occupied by people with no awareness of their God. The people of Judah have been dispersed, taken off in chains, and left to wonder where God is in all of this. Many of their prophets had earlier warned them that their behavior reeked of idolatry and injustice, and in exile they are paying the price. Now the prophets must console and comfort God's people and prepare them to invest themselves more wholeheartedly in the covenant God made with them.

The promise of unshakable peace must have sounded like a fantasy. Surely we can relate to that wonderment: How can God speak of peace when all around us there's evidence of unrest and violence? While we wish God would wave a wand and make it all cease (certainly God is capable of this), God chooses to work through our efforts. Each step that decreases anxiety is a step toward peace. Each time we choose forgiveness instead of retaliation is a choice for peace. Each effort made to create a just world is a part of peace-building. I like to imagine God using each of these building blocks of peace to construct an unshakable house to shelter all.

Meditation: In a world where violence abounds in our many sources for gathering news, it may feel naïve to believe in the peace that God promises; evidence seems to point to the contrary. It is our task not only to choose peace in small and large ways by our decisions and activities, but to also uncover the evidence of God's love and peace that are right in our midst. Speak about acts of mercy and forgiveness, share information about agencies that pursue peaceful paths to justice, and pray for the courage to promote peace wherever there is discord.

Prayer: Jesus, Prince of Peace, may your coming among us continue to signal the priority of peace and love. Help us to trust in your promises and invest ourselves in your divine agenda.

December 17: Friday of the Third Week of Advent

Follow the Way of Justice

Readings: Gen 49:2, 8-10; Matt 1:1-17

Scripture:
Justice shall flourish in his time, and fullness of peace for
   ever. (Ps 72:7)

Reflection: Many of us in the Western world equate justice
with revenge or punishment. The Old Testament principle
of "an eye for an eye" found in Exodus 21 and Deuteronomy
19 sounds reasonable when we consider that vigilante justice
would have demanded more. But the broader biblical ideal
of justice is even more demanding. In fact, tomorrow's reading from Jeremiah will identify the Messiah as "our justice,"
telling us that God wants to stretch us even further. Just as
God restores and rebuilds us when we fail, God desires that
we do the same for each other.

Jesus was very familiar with the law that limited punishment to fit the crime. In the gospels, he says, "You have heard
that it was said, 'An eye for an eye,'" but then he continues,
"But I say to you . . ." For Jesus, even justice that is fair
punishment does not go far enough. Instead, Jesus insists
that we turn the other cheek, that we love our enemies, and
that we do good to those who hate us. This is a very tall
order, and for many, an extremely impractical one. But, have
we tried it? Have we found a way in our personal lives to

restore a broken relationship rather than end it? Have we considered ways to bring healing to the victims of crime as well as the perpetrators, what some call restorative justice? At the core of the Christian idea of justice is the belief that each person possesses God-given dignity, and it is that dignity that requires us to do more than simply punish without a pathway to restoration and healing.

Meditation: Justice demands that we are accountable for the way we live our lives, and that rights and responsibilities go hand in hand. Our faith communities are the perfect settings to explore ways to lovingly resolve conflicts, to seek justice for victims of crime that will be lasting, and to consider how to rebuild broken relationships. How might these conversations take place in your parish? In your family? What is most challenging about the teaching of Jesus to go beyond an "eye for an eye"?

Prayer: Jesus, O Wisdom Incarnate, direct us in your ways. Provide the path that leads our families to greater love and our civic communities to greater harmony. In times of unrest, give us the wisdom to bend to your will and to uphold your justice in all our dealings.

Pursue Wisdom

Readings: Jer 23:5-8; Matt 1:18-25

Scripture:
"Joseph, son of David, do not be afraid to take Mary your
wife into your home. For it is through the Holy Spirit
that this child has been conceived in her." (Matt 1:20)

Reflection: By all cultural and religious standards of the
time, Joseph would have been justified in ending his commitment to Mary. Actually, by law, he could have had her
stoned to death. Her pregnancy would have been a source
of shame; he was not the father of the child, and they had
not yet lived together and sealed their betrothal. He searched
for wisdom, which led him to the notion of a quiet divorce.
In the context of the time, this decision is admirable and
shows a great deal of restraint and even respect. But God's
wisdom needed more growth in Joseph. It came in the form
of a dream, the voice of an angel urging extraordinary courage from Joseph, and profound trust.

My own search for wisdom in life's inevitable sticky situations has never found an angel speaking to me in a dream.
Instead, I am assisted by faith-filled friends, the writing of
spiritual guides, the words of Scripture, and the grace of the
sacraments. I have found wisdom if I slow down, if I am
persistent, and if I am open. The evidence of God's wisdom

presents itself in many forms—with deep peace while making a life-changing decision, with joy in unexpected circumstances, with profound sorrow finding out I have hurt someone, with fervor in taking action to correct an injustice, and with quiet resolve in the midst of fear or anxiety. Joseph speaks to me as a powerful witness to the virtue of listening and then doing the right and loving thing.

Meditation: I've often found myself seeking wisdom for my life or in a difficult situation. But I'm not always prepared to receive the wisdom God offers. It's been my experience that God's wisdom rarely allows us to do what is comfortable. It asks us to be pliable rather than rigid, to be ready to move rather than stay in place. "If any of you lacks wisdom," writes James (1:5), "he should ask God who gives to all generously and ungrudgingly." And then be prepared to think and do differently.

Prayer: O Lord of Israel, deliver your people from harm. Give us the desire to seek you, and the resolve to follow where you lead us. Like Joseph, in times of uncertainty or anguish, may we hear your voice.

FOURTH WEEK OF ADVENT

Learn to Trust in God

Readings: Mic 5:1-4a; Heb 10:5-10; Luke 1:39-45

Scripture:
"Blessed are you who believed that what was spoken to
  you by the Lord would be fulfilled." (Luke 1:45)

Reflection: One of my young nephews was taking swim
lessons, but had not become brave enough to leave the edges
of the pool or push off from the wide steps that went down
into the water. On vacation I was determined to get him more
comfortable with the water and with using his body to actually swim. Every day we started on the steps and every day
bit by bit he would come farther into the water to reach me
as I slowly inched away toward the deep end. By the end of
our week in the pool he was swimming like a fish. He had
to learn to trust me, and to trust himself. The water would
have engulfed him without that element of trust.

Today's joy-filled gospel reading is a testament to trust.
Elizabeth and Mary each experienced God's radical interven-
tion in their lives. Both women were unlikely candidates to
give birth to children; one was past childbearing years and
the other not yet ready. They trusted in God's word, and
surely had to learn to trust in themselves and their experiences of God. When Elizabeth blesses Mary for believing in
God's promise, she is not talking so much about Mary's intel-

lectual consent as she is about a gut-level trust that allowed Mary to place her future in God's hands. The waters of fear could have pulled them under—fear of gossip, fear about the future, self-doubt—but their experience of God allowed Mary and Elizabeth to trust God enough to enter the deep waters of God's abiding love and care.

Meditation: From the time of creation, God has been inviting us into a profound relationship of trust, which is the core of what it means to believe in God. We are called to trust that God is with us long before we are called to consent to doctrine. In fact, consenting to the teachings of our faith only makes sense in the context of a trusting relationship with God. There we discover God to be Lord of our lives, transforming our uncertainty into a sure foundation.

Prayer: O Root of Jesse's Stem, promise of God from the least among the tribes of Israel, flower once again among your people. Put to rest our enemies—uncertainty, fear, and doubt—and raise to life a spirit of trust in your power and goodness.

December 20: Monday of the Fourth Week of Advent

Say Yes to God's Grace

Readings: Isa 7:10-14; Luke 1:26-38

Scripture:
"Do not be afraid, Mary, for you have found favor with
   God." (Luke 1:30)

Reflection: The teacher's pet, the golden child, the priority
traveler. We have so many ways of saying that someone is
singled out and receiving special treatment. At first blush,
that might be what some hear in the angel Gabriel's words
to Mary. She is certainly being singled out, but in Scripture
being favored is not equivalent to being the favorite.

Mary is being told that she is like others in the Bible for
whom divine favor (also translated as grace) meant great
responsibility. Genesis tells us Noah was favored and his job
was to save creation from a great flood. Also in Genesis, the
patriarch Joseph is favored by God and he ends up being sold
into slavery, rising in the ranks of Pharaoh's servants, and
then saving his brothers who originally did him such harm.
In Exodus, Moses is favored by God, which entailed match-
ing wits with Pharaoh, forcing the release of the slaves, wandering in the desert for years, and never even getting to enter
the Promised Land. The first book of Samuel tells the story
of Hannah and her son Samuel, for whom divine favor meant
speaking God's word to those who did not want to hear it.

Mary knows the stories of these ancestors. She has to know that her role in God's plan will not be easy. She is of the house of David, of the tribe of Benjamin, from whom the prophets announced God's anointed would come. She will need trust and courage to respond to God's favor.

Meditation: Most of us will not be visited by an angel, but all of us are given some responsibility in the plan of salvation. Through our baptisms, God has already equipped us to use our passions and personalities, our talents and treasures, to say yes to building the kingdom of God. That does not mean that our "yes" will always be easy, but it does mean that we have access to the grace (or "favor") of God that Mary experienced in a unique way. How will we say yes in this season? Where will we share our abilities?

Prayer: O Key of David, open our hearts to the grace of God working in us and among us. May our lives reflect to others the joy of saying yes to your limitless love and mercy.

December 21: Tuesday of the Fourth Week of Advent

Share Your Joys

Readings: Song 2:8-14 or Zeph 3:14-18a; Luke 1:39-45

Scripture:
Mary set out in those days and traveled to the hill country
in haste to a town of Judah, where she entered the house
of Zechariah and greeted Elizabeth. (Luke 1:39)

Reflection: When my sister was pregnant with her first child,
she and her husband were living halfway across the country.
They would be traveling home for Christmas and made a
plan to share their news with us when we were all gathered
together. They devised a game of sorts and in the process
revealed the good news. I'll never forget the surprise, the
disbelief, the joy, and the tears of happiness that permeated
that moment of revelation and endured throughout their
visit. This proclamation of good news was a time of grace
for our family.

When I picture Mary traveling to visit Elizabeth, I picture
the kind of reunion that is filled to the brim with all the same
emotions we felt that Thanksgiving years ago. There was no
way to communicate the good news except in a personal
visit. Perhaps both women were the subject of gossip in their
towns. The pity once felt for an older woman like Elizabeth
who was barren was now probably transformed into specu-
lation. And Mary's pregnancy at such a young age and with-

out benefit of living with her husband surely raised eyebrows. Now these women could support one another and share their experiences of God. It was a trip worth making.

Meditation: Many artistic renderings of the visitation of Mary to Elizabeth show two women huddled together, perhaps whispering, or laughing, or weeping. These women appear to be conspiring, and how appropriate if we know the word is literally "to breathe together" (con = with; spire = breath or spirit). They are aware that God's breath, present at creation, is present in the creation of the children in their wombs. Their laughter and their tears are signs of the very breath of God in this moment of grace. With whom do we share our experiences of God's life in us?

Prayer: O Jesus, Radiant Dawn, fill this day with opportunities to experience your presence. Provide faithful friends and relatives with whom we can share the good news of your life in us. In these waning days of Advent, help us to be joyful in sharing the news of your coming.

Rediscover Awe of the Lord

Readings: 1 Sam 1:24-28; Luke 1:46-56

Scripture:
"He has mercy on those who fear him
   in every generation.
He has shown the strength of his arm. . . ." (Luke 1:50-51a)

Reflection: One of my college professors, a brilliant historian, father to seven or eight children, read the *Summa* of Thomas Aquinas at night before retiring, loved gardening, and was a superb storyteller. He was what I would call a Renaissance man. He never tired of learning, and instilled in us that same desire. He had complete control of the classroom and demanded the best from us in our discussions and writing assignments. I have a clear memory of this intellectual giant assigning us to read Robert Bolt's play, *A Man for All Seasons.* One day in class we became aware that our professor was in tears as he read a scene from the prison cell of St. Thomas More. We, too, were caught up in the depth of More's sense of right and wrong. And we were in awe of our professor who evoked such a deep awareness.

The fear of the Lord that Mary speaks of is this kind of awe. It serves as a hinge between God's mercy and God's might. Awe is the only truly human response once we grasp that God who is all powerful also stoops to us to extend kindness and healing. We stand in awe at God's ability to hold together two characteristics that seem to be opposites: power and compassion. Mary reflects this insight in her prayer. She would see this ability to hold together opposites in the life of her son, Jesus, who would set a high bar for obedience at the same time that he extended love and forgiveness.

Meditation: The Canticle of Mary (the *Magnificat*) appears only here in our cycle of readings for Mass. While it is not proclaimed as a gospel reading on any Sunday when most of the church is gathered, it is a key element of the Liturgy of the Hours in Evening Prayer (also known as Vespers). Just as Mary reviews what God has done for her and for God's people throughout history, each evening we can also pray with Mary using her words. It will renew in us the sense of awe and wonder at God's work in our lives and throughout the world.

Prayer: O Desire of All Nations, instill in us a pure sense of wonder as we contemplate how you fashioned the human heart to desire you. In these final days of Advent, enable us to give witness to your mighty deeds and your marvelous mercy.

December 23: Thursday of the Fourth Week of Advent

Prepare the Way of the Lord

Readings: Mal 3:1-4, 23-24; Luke 1:57-66

Scripture:
Lo, I am sending my messenger
   to prepare the way before me. . . . (Mal 3:1)

Reflection: The church sees in our readings today the opportunity to highlight the role that John the Baptist will play in preparing the way for Jesus. In the reading from Malachi, the prophet's words are preparing the people for the coming of God's messenger who will purify them. And then, several centuries later, Luke describes the birth of John the Baptist, the child who will become an itinerant prophet, preaching and baptizing for repentance in advance of Jesus' public ministry. The prophet says that the day of the Lord will be a great and terrible day. If we're paying attention, that would sound a little ominous.

The prophet Malachi lived at a time when it seems chaos and corruption were the order of the day. The book that bears his name describes numerous religious abuses and violations of the covenant with God. The day of the Lord will provide a reckoning that will not go so well for those who ignore God's desires and refuse to respond to the call for repentance. So, the "terrible day of the Lord" is the day of decision, not when God decides who is in and who is out but when we, by our own decisions, decide whom we will serve.

In these few days before Christmas we are being reminded to prepare the way of the Lord in our lives, so that the day of the Lord's coming will not be a time of terror but of rejoicing.

Meditation: The prophets, from Amos to John the Baptist, invite us to imagine a world in harmony with God's mercy and justice and faithfulness. The Scriptures give us language and images to prepare our hearts to receive not just a child born in a manger, but to receive the adult Christ who challenges cultural standards and dares us to follow him. Where is the way of the Lord leading us? How shall we walk along this way?

Prayer: Jesus, you are Emmanuel, God With Us. We are grateful for those who have paved the way for you to enter our lives. Be with us as we respond to your generous mercy. May our response of obedience be a sign of our love for you.

December 24: Friday of the Fourth Week of Advent
(Christmas Eve)

Experience Salvation through Forgiveness

Readings: 2 Sam 7:1-5, 8b-12, 14a, 16; Luke 1:67-79

Scripture:
"[Y]ou will go before the Lord to prepare his way,
    to give his people knowledge of salvation
    by the forgiveness of their sins." (Luke 1:76b-77)

Reflection: Forgiveness is one of the most powerful of human experiences, potent for its mental health benefits and more importantly for what it teaches us about the salvation God offers to us. On this eve of Christmas, we are compelled to consider the kind of God who wants us to come to experience salvation through the gift of forgiveness. One example comes to mind immediately.

In 2006, five young girls were shot to death and five more seriously wounded in a one-room Amish schoolhouse in rural Pennsylvania. The shooter then took his own life. Scenes from that horrible day played over and over in the news, not only because of the horror that was experienced on that day, but for the unbelievable unity in forgiveness that was offered by the Amish community, especially to the parents of the shooter. The parents of those murdered went to the home of the shooter's parents to offer forgiveness and comfort. They attended not only the funerals of their children but the funeral of the shooter. They embraced forgiveness in dramatic, heart-wrenching fashion. Their work of forgiveness began immediately, but doing that work is not a once and for all proposition. They continue to do the work that healing requires.

The forgiveness offered by the Amish community is revelatory. It unveils what they have embraced in their spiritual journey, and speaks volumes about who God is to them and how they experience salvation.

Meditation: Mahatma Gandhi, the prophet of peace in India, said that it is not possible for the weak to forgive because forgiveness is the attribute of the strong. What a strong and powerful God we have who sends his son into our world to offer forgiveness as a pathway to salvation! The child we await this night is himself the Prince of Peace, the bringer of forgiveness and healing.

Prayer: O come, O come, Emmanuel. You are God With Us, giver of freedom. Help us to accept the forgiveness you offer and to extend this gift to others so that they may know you too.

SEASON OF CHRISTMAS

December 25: The Nativity of the Lord (Christmas)

Unwrap Beauty

Readings:
VIGIL: Isa 62:1-5; Acts 13:16-17, 22-25; Matt 1:1-25 *or* 1:18-25
NIGHT: Isa 9:1-6; Titus 2:11-14; Luke 2:1-14
DAWN: Isa 62:11-12; Titus 3:4-7; Luke 2:15-20
DAY: Isa 52:7-10; Heb 1:1-6; John 1:1-18 *or* 1:1-5, 9-14

Scripture:
. . . [God] has spoken to us through the Son, . . .
   who is the refulgence of his glory,
      the very imprint of his being,
and who sustains all things by his mighty word.
   (Heb 1:2, 3)

Reflection: I am drawn to beauty—color, movement, language, sound. Classic works of art and simple blossoms growing out of cracks capture my attention. The sounds of a storm can carve out a strange stillness in me, just as easily as the trickle of water in a stream. Beauty, for me, creates necessary pauses in my life that allow me simply to be in the moment, putting aside productivity and anxiety. I am drawn to participate in that beauty in some way: to dance, or sing, or plant, or write. The coming of Jesus feels to me like a wild burst of beauty, a thundering beauty that requires rapt attention to the moment of God's coming.

The passage from Hebrews captures some of this sense for me. God has burst onto the scene in the birth of a child, a wild and precious life gasping for air, announcing his coming with that cry of arrival that every parent knows to be good news. This child communicates who God is: creator and sustainer. From his birth to his death he carries the very imprint of God's being, a profound beauty that draws us into wonder and response. Jesus, the refulgence of God's glory, draws us this day into brilliant light.

Meditation: Christmas Day is often filled with expectations about creating the perfect memory for our families, or trying to recover those memories if we are not with others we love. Maybe we can put aside just for a few moments the expectation of anything except discovering the beauty of God's coming. Whether alone or with others, where might we find signs of this beauty waiting to be unwrapped?

Prayer: O Jesus, radiant dawn of our world, herald of beauty, open our eyes to see you.

O Jesus, Word made flesh, voice of God, open our minds to contemplate you.

O Jesus, redeemer of all, hand of salvation, open our hearts to love you.

December 26: The Holy Family of Jesus, Mary, and Joseph

Become a Holy Family

Readings: Sir 3:2-6, 12-14 *or* 1 Sam 1:20-22, 24-28; Col 3:12-21 *or* 3:12-17 *or* 1 John 3:1-2, 21-24; Luke 2:41-52

Scripture:
"I prayed for this child, and the LORD granted my request."
(1 Sam 1:27)

Reflection: So many couples are unable to conceive for such a wide variety of reasons. One friend of mine had suffered through many miscarriages before carrying a child to term. When their daughter was born, the birth announcements began with the words of Hannah, "I prayed for this child. . . ." Another couple whom I know also tried without success for many years to conceive a child, and when they adopted their first child, their birth announcement contained the same passage from First Samuel. How simply and beautifully these ancient words express what so many hold in their hearts: the desire for the blessing of a child.

What strikes me is that praying for our children is such a fundamental part of what it means to be an adult. Hannah prayed that she would conceive a child, and I am quite certain she also prayed for her son, Samuel, to grow to maturity in the ways of God. Mothers and fathers, stepparents, aunts and uncles, grandparents and friends, share with God their concerns about raising children, and their hopes and dreams for their children to find purpose. In the most fundamental way, we simply present our children to God, knowing that God loves them with abandon. When the inevitable challenges of family life take their toll, we hope we have given them a firm foundation. It takes a great deal of work to be a family; it takes a great deal of trust and prayer to be a holy family.

Meditation: On this feast of the Holy Family, consider that holiness is not about perfection. If that were the case, no family could be holy. Holiness begins in knowing that God has set us apart for a purpose, not just individually but in the midst of community. In the chaos and imperfection of family life, we have the opportunity to learn about our gifts and talents, our temperaments, what our callings may be, and how to respond to needs in our world. We have the opportunity to pray not just for each other but with each other, grounding our lives in the presence of God.

Prayer: O God, you call your people to holiness. Come and take up residence in the lives of our families, giving us opportunities to respond to your love in the ways we love one another. Multiply your goodness in our lives so that where there is division, we may be instruments of your healing.

December 27: Saint John, Apostle and Evangelist

Give Witness

Readings: 1 John 1:1-4; John 20:1a, 2-8

Scripture:
. . . what we have seen and heard
we proclaim now to you,
so that you too may have fellowship with us. . . . (1 John
1:3)

Reflection: One of the great joys of my life is the gift of enduring and meaningful friendships. My best friends from childhood, along with a few friends made while away in college and graduate school, are still an important part of my life. I treasure them, along with the friends who have graced my life during my years of ministry. We support one another through trials, cheer each other through accomplishments, and challenge one another to widen our perspectives. On more than one occasion, a friend has helped me to see Christ at work in my life and in the lives of those I love.

When I think about how the First Letter of John opens, I cannot help but think about the power of relationships, especially friendships. Where do we turn when we want to share good news? We find a way to reach our friends and family; we want to share with them what is important to us and what we hope will be important to them as well. In the First Letter of John, the writer offers testimony about Jesus, the Word of Life, to any who will hear his message. He is gathering them into the circle of friendship he now experiences with Christ and wishes for them to experience too.

The friends we need are those who share what they have seen and heard as God acts in their lives. We need to be that friend for others as well.

Meditation: The opening verses of the First Letter of John says basically that the writer has seen God at work with his own eyes and touched the evidence of God's work. He wants to make clear that while we sometimes search for evidence of God, it is not all that hard to find. Listen to those who know God, who have experienced Christ alive in them. Ask for the grace to welcome the light of Christ through their witness. How will the bonds of friendship with others lead us to Christ again and again?

Prayer: You, Lord, give us friends to journey with us through this world. Fill our friendships with steady love, firm truth, and the joy of walking in your ways. May our witness to each other build up the Body of Christ.

December 28: The Holy Innocents, Martyrs

Be Like Joseph

Readings: 1 John 1:5–2:2; Matt 2:13-18

Scripture:
Joseph rose and took the child and his mother by night
   and departed for Egypt. (Matt 2:14)

Reflection: I am sad to report that every single day in my
adult life I have found in the media a report or two about
children who are in danger. Children go hungry at an alarm-
ing rate and show up in classrooms with hunger pangs instead of the curiosity to learn. The foster care system is
overloaded and under-supervised. Children sometimes van-
ish never to be found. Some children never see the light of
day. Child abuse occurs more often than we want to admit.
Children are impacted by gun violence, as well as drug and
alcohol abuse by the adults in their lives. The list could go
on and on.

On this feast of the Holy Innocents, we remember the
devastating jealousy of King Herod and his monstrous plan
to eliminate any future threat to his power. We lament the
children lost to violence in ancient Bethlehem. But we would
do well to remember that the suffering of innocent children
has remained a constant in this world. This year, let us focus
on Joseph, and all those like him who perceive danger and
take action to protect the innocent: teachers and school coun-

selors who find ways to intervene; school and shelter cooks who provide food for the hungry; neighbors who keep watch for signs of neglect; medical professionals who offer their services to those without access to regular health care; officers of the law, social workers, and judges who try to determine how best to care for children in danger; young people who offer friendship, laughter, and inclusion. Our world needs more Josephs.

Meditation: From all indications, Joseph and Mary were people of prayer as well as action. Their flight to Egypt was not just desperation but was a response to God's direction. Let us do our best to educate ourselves about what endangers young lives in our world today. Take this information to prayer and ask what you may do to be part of providing a safer world for those who are innocent, who through no fault of their own find themselves fearful and lost. Where might each of us be able to make a difference?

Prayer: O God, protector of the innocent, remind us of the sacred image that each person carries. Stir our conscience so that we truly lament the suffering in our world. Then prod us to action, and give us the courage to protect your littlest ones.

December 29:
Fifth Day within the Octave of the Nativity of the Lord

Obey God's Commands

Readings: 1 John 2:3-11; Luke 2:22-35

Scripture:
The way we may be sure that we know Jesus is to keep his
commandments. (1 John 2:3)

Reflection: A former student, now married and the mother
of two children in grade school, astounds me. She and another young mother in our parish saw a need and stepped
in to address it. They created a ministry that teams up with
a local homeless shelter; the shelter works to provide housing
for their clients, and the group in our parish helps them to
settle in with furnishings and touches that make a simple
apartment into a home.

Stephanie and her team are responding to a need and in
doing so are responding to the commands of Jesus to love
one another and care for the least among us. In the process
these folks experience a sense of their own dignity, and
friendships blossom. This ministry requires an awful lot of
organizing. Donations have to be gathered, and sorted and
stored efficiently. Volunteers have to be informed and available for the move-in day. Trucks have to loaded and un-
loaded. Obeying the commandments requires more than
good intentions.

Loving God and loving neighbor require a commitment of our whole being. We cannot stand in awe at the manger scene and then be unmoved when others have no place to lay their heads. The New Testament letters, such as our letter today from John, reveal that the level of commitment required to love God and others requires constant instruction and encouragement.

Meditation: Far from restricting us, the commands of God actually free us to grow into our identity as Christians. It makes sense that the God who created us knows what will enable us to grow to maturity and empower us to become friends with God. Doing the loving thing will not always be easy, but it will always be fruitful. Living a loving life produces generosity, gratitude, self-understanding, integrity, and greater trust in God. In the routines of our daily lives, where might God be asking for a greater commitment to love?

Prayer: Jesus, your life taught us what it means to love God with all your heart and to love your neighbor as yourself. Every day, increase our desire to love as you love and to find our deepest identity in responding to the love you already share with us.

December 30:
Sixth Day within the Octave of the Nativity of the Lord

Recognize Jesus in the Temple

Readings: 1 John 2:12-17; Luke 2:36-40

Scripture:
[Anna] never left the temple, but worshiped night and day
with fasting and prayer. (Luke 2:37)

Reflection: When the story of the presentation of Jesus in the
temple is proclaimed in the Sunday liturgy, a shorter option
is available and it skips over Anna entirely. Thankfully, the
reading for daily Mass offers her brief story in its entirety.
Widowed and into her 80s, Anna provides a wonderful example of faithfulness. You might be thinking that the average
person cannot be expected to be at the temple (or in the
church) night and day fasting and praying, and you'd be
right. But what if the temple that we visit is the temple of
our hearts? And the fasting we do is fasting from the patterns
of sinfulness in our lives? And the constancy of our praying
is intentionally offering to God our days and all that they
hold?

St. Paul wrote to the church in Corinth, "Do you not know
that you are the temple of God, and that the Spirit of God
dwells in you?" (1 Cor 3:16). During the pandemic of 2019–
2021 we were given the opportunity to discover once again
that God always abides in his people, whether or not we

could physically participate in public worship. Reading the Scriptures, making acts of spiritual communion, online worship, and personal prayer became our rhythm. Of course, this is not new to the large number of people who, because of disease or aging, are unable to join the worshiping community on a regular basis. God dwells within us, and we meet God in the silence of our hearts, in the hubbub of our days, and in acts of penance and service.

Meditation: We need models of faithfulness in our lives, people like Anna whose constancy in the sight of all is itself a witness to trusting in God's goodness. We also need to discover that within us we can visit God's temple with the same constancy. We need to know that the desire to find God in our midst is itself part of the process that leads us inward to encounter, to repentance, and to hope. Make it a point to find Jesus in the temple that is your life.

Prayer: Jesus, your presentation at the Jerusalem temple was the sign of fulfillment that Anna awaited. Help us to wait faithfully and with purpose for the ways you will appear in our lives. Give us the gift of constancy in our spiritual practices so that our hope for your reign will be fulfilled.

December 31:
Seventh Day within the Octave of the Nativity of the Lord

Raise a Toast to Life

Readings: 1 John 2:18-21; John 1:1-18

Scripture:
What came to be through him was life,
and this life was the light of the human race. . . .
(John 1:4)

Reflection: L'chaim, to life! In the classic story *Fiddler on the Roof*, a family patriarch, Tevye, struggles with maintaining the family's Jewish identity and traditions in the midst of anti-Semitic policies in early twentieth-century Russia. Audiences, me included, have long loved the production for its poignancy, its music and dancing, and its beloved characters. In its most recognized song, Tevye raises a toast to life, even as he says it "has a way of confusing us, blessing and bruising us." Who hasn't known this to be true?

The Gospel of John raises a similar toast to life, praising the enfleshed Word of God who dares to bring light into a world where darkness lingers like an unwelcome intruder at a banquet. Into the commotion of family life, God comes as light. Into the fears of waning health, God comes as light. Into the disgrace of racism, God comes as light. Into the scandal of violence, God comes as light. When light arrives in a space, darkness flees. Christ, our light, continues to shine brightly, inviting us to illumine those places where shadows linger. We carry the lantern of his light, pulling back the curtains, calling out, "To life!"

Meditation: As this calendar year comes to a close, perhaps we could consider how the light of Christ has helped us to identify the shadows that remain in our world. In this past year, what has bruised us, left us hurting a bit from contact? When have we found ourselves turning in prayer for guidance and strength? What has helped us dig deep for the blessing of strength and resiliency? These are the places where God chooses to bring light through the indwelling of his son in us. When we begin to see even slivers of light emerging in these shadowy places, perhaps when we bring that light ourselves, let us raise a toast to the author of life, the source of light.

Prayer: Christ our light, brighten this weary world with your continuing generous mercy.

Word made flesh, teach us to search for your truth and live in its light.

Giver of life, send us forth with renewed energy to bless this world.

January 1: Solemnity of Mary, the Holy Mother of God

Desire Peace

Readings: Num 6:22-27; Gal 4:4-7; Luke 2:16-21

Scripture:
The Lord look upon you kindly and
    give you peace! (Num 6:26)

Reflection: I have a friend who often ponders along these lines: "If an alien was to show up, what would it make of all of this?" This friend is usually trying to make sense of something he's seen on the news, or a situation at his workplace. His point is that we sometimes need to step back and see things from the point of view of an interested but uninvolved observer. In the past year or so, I've wondered about what an observer would make of us as a people by simply reading our posts on social media. Would that observer find evidence of a thoughtful people, a wise community, a people who desire peace? Sadly, I think not. While various social media platforms have allowed us to stay in touch, and to share ideas and information, they have also allowed us to become more reactive than responsive or more knee-jerk than thoughtful.

The blessing found in the book of Numbers reminds me that God desires peace, the kind of peace that settles in the midst of a people in the form of wholeness and justice. All of us who profess to be Christians have an obligation, it seems to me, to build the kind of environment where this desire for peace would be obvious to that outside observer. The words we use and the groups we support provide an opportunity to give witness to our priorities. The question is whether we are willing to slow down enough to do as Mary did and reflect on God's message in our hearts.

Meditation: January 1 is the Solemnity of Mary, Mother of God. Across the Christian world it is also the World Day of Peace. I'd call this a happy coincidence, or better yet, a graced connection. The mother of the Prince of Peace teaches us to be reflective before reacting, to ponder in our hearts before words pass our lips or appear on the screen in social media. Mary teaches us to conform our desires to those of God. Do my desires reflect the desire of God for peace? Do my words and actions add to the well of peace from which we may all draw water? Perhaps taking steps toward peace might make it on a short list of resolutions for the year ahead.

Prayer: Loving Lord, Prince of Peace, continue to shape our minds and hearts. May our words build up rather than tear down. May we identify obstacles to peace in such a way that they draw people to you.

Mary, Mother of God, intercede for us as we learn to imitate your son.

EPIPHANY AND BAPTISM OF THE LORD

January 2: The Epiphany of the Lord

Become a Traveling Companion

Readings: Isa 60:1-6; Eph 3:2-3a, 5-6; Matt 2:1-12

Scripture:
"Go and search diligently for the child." (Matt 2:8)

Reflection: In most parishes where I have worshiped, the three magi do not appear anywhere near the creche until Christmas Day, eventually entering our peripheral vision. Day by day they journey closer to the manger until on Epiphany they finally arrive. I have friends who allow their children to move the magi around the house each day as they search for the baby whose small family is huddled in a stable. It isn't by magic that the eastern sages appear in Bethlehem; they are responding to a celestial sign and have been traveling in search of a child whom they know in some way addresses the hopes of all.

The feast of Epiphany highlights the story of the magi as part of the continuation of the Christmas event. If those who hear of Jesus' birth do not yet understand its significance, his identity is further revealed in the coming of Gentiles to bring gifts and to humble themselves in his presence. Matthew includes the story in his gospel to emphasize that salvation is available even to those outside of Israel's covenant relationship with God.

You and I know many people who are searching for something. Some want to find a deeper meaning to their lives, some want to find the right career path, and others want to find freedom from whatever binds them. By our own drawing near to Jesus, we have something to offer them in their search—not a pat answer to their questions, but companionship on the journey of discovering the love of God that gives meaning to everything else.

Meditation: Sometimes we have the impression that having found Jesus, our search is complete. Of course, we're always challenged to grow in our relationship with Jesus and our understanding of his kingdom. It's possible, too, that another search begins: the search for how best to use the gifts we have been given to bring others to Jesus. We want people to remark to themselves, "I'd like to know what he's got that keeps him going," or "I've got to get to know her and see what makes her life so joyful." We have opportunities every day to reveal to others the person we know who began life in a manger in Bethlehem.

Prayer: Jesus, we know that your light shines for all to see. Help us to be trusted companions to those searching for you, whether or not they know where the journey will lead. Give us direction, keep us humble, and fill us with joy.

Repent

Readings: 1 John 3:22–4:6; Matt 4:12-17, 23-25

Scripture:
"Repent, for the Kingdom of heaven is at hand."
   (Matt 4:17)

Reflection: I can recall realizing that when the gospels talked about the kingdom of God or the kingdom of heaven, it was not someplace far off and removed from this world. The kingdom Jesus speaks of and invites us to share in is "at hand," in our midst, near, among us! I was in high school and I wondered how in the world it could be true when it was clear that war was never off the front pages, corruption in government was a daily occurrence, poor people were still poor, and people I loved still became gravely ill. If the kingdom Jesus speaks of brings glad tidings to the poor and healing to the sick and peace that passes understanding, where was the evidence?

   One key to finding that evidence is removing what clouds my vision. I discovered the need for repentance. Both John the Baptist and Jesus call out, "Repent," and I've come to believe that beating one's chest is not exactly what they had in mind. The classic definition is that to repent is to turn from sin. Think of physically turning in a new direction, turning to gain a fresh perspective, turning so that harmful habits cannot easily be picked up again. When we make these kinds of turns, we notice that the solutions begin with each follower of Christ. We become the evidence of the kingdom of heaven. We begin to realize that God's kingdom takes root ever more fully with each resolve to use the grace given us to help change the world.

Meditation: Am I a glad tiding to the poor? Do I engage with people who do not have access to the things I take for granted? Am I committed to understanding the dynamics of poverty in our world, and am I willing to live simply? Am I a glad tiding to those who are ill or depressed or lonely? How does my presence bring the light of Christ into the lives of others? Am I a glad tiding in politically charged atmospheres or do I add to the chaos and mistrust? Do I value the things that Jesus values, taking these values into the marketplace and the civic world? From what is God asking me to turn in order to receive the grace I need to see the kingdom and to be an agent of its coming?

Prayer: Jesus, bringer of God's kingdom into our midst, help us turn to you and away from what is not of you. May the repentance we offer day to day lead to a greater investment in bringing your kingdom ever more fully into view.

January 4: Saint Elizabeth Ann Seton, Religious

Respond to Love

Readings: 1 John 4:7-10; Mark 6:34-44

Scripture:
. . . for God is love. (1 John 4:8)

Reflection: The history of the world has been filled with efforts to define God. Personally, I think we could have stopped centuries ago and spent these generations pondering the profound truth from the First Letter of John: God is love.

Of course, love only exists in relationship to another. And that means that God's very nature is about relationship. We speak of the loving bond between Father, Son, and Holy Spirit to speak about God. And then, wonder of wonders, we are invited into that relationship. To say that we love God is to say that we are responding to the love that God has first shown us. To say that we love others is to say that God in us loves those who are also the product of God's loving intent. We respond best to God when we surrender to love. This means we choose love, and we keep choosing it.

The feeding of the multitude that is today's gospel story is reported by all four evangelists. It shows us in word and deed that Jesus expresses love in practical ways. He is moved with compassion for those who seek him out, and he satisfies their hungers both spiritually and physically. This is a feel-good story, right? But it is also a story that twists a bit, asking us to follow Jesus to learn what love requires. Ultimately the bread he will share will be the bread of his own life.

Meditation: God is love. This simple statement sums up who God is and how God acts. It invites us into relationship and provides the motivation for our actions. Being made in God's image, we, too, should be about love—love that consoles, love that provides, love that corrects, love that raises up, love that shares sorrow, love that repents, love that rebuilds. Will others know we follow the God of love when they come to know us?

Prayer: We are grateful, O God, to worship you, the God of love. May love animate our relationships, motivate our actions, and always direct us to love you more day by day. As you feed us with your very life, may we spend our lives feeding the hungers of those around us.

Surrender to One Who Knows the Seas

Readings: 1 John 4:11-18; Mark 6:45-52

Scripture:
[Jesus] got into the boat with them and the wind died
down. (Mark 6:51)

Reflection: I know a young single mother who struggles
with financial obligations, and who has spent the past few
years fighting the good fight for sobriety. She is funny, but
she is also wounded. She is diligent, but she is also stubborn.
Often, when she says, "I'm okay," her voice betrays her and
I know that she is very much not okay. She is like many of
us, struggling with her humanity and experiencing setbacks
almost as often as achievements. I marvel that she holds it
all together. When I pray for her, sometimes I picture her in
a rowboat on a stormy lake, struggling to fight against the
winds she faces, working hard to keep water out of her boat.
And I simply ask Jesus to please get in that boat, to calm
those winds and let the sun peek through the clouds. Perhaps
I want that for her because I'm not sure how to calm the
winds for her, and I'm quite sure she wouldn't want me to
rescue her anyway.

There is strength in knowing our limitations, and great
wisdom in surrendering to a greater power. My friend has
shown that to me in her life, and the gospel tells us the same

truth. The apostles were incapable of calming a storm, but they knew enough to welcome Jesus into their boat, even before they knew for sure that with him on board the winds would die down.

Meditation: Use your imagination to picture whatever trials you are having as a storm threatening to overtake your small boat. Do you feel alone? Frightened? Exhausted? Are you willing to let someone else take the helm? Willing to take on a passenger who might have the power you need?

Prayer: We turn to you, Faithful One, when our days are overwhelming and our nights restless. We reach out to you who know each of us well, and ask you to calm our inner storms. Give us room to breathe, to regroup, and to face the days ahead with confidence that you are with us.

Don't Stop at Wonder

Readings: 1 John 4:19–5:4; Luke 4:14-22a

Scripture:
[A]ll spoke highly of [Jesus] and were amazed at the
gracious words that came from his mouth. (Luke 4:22)

Reflection: We speak of amazement and usually intend to
communicate a sense of wonder or surprise. Interestingly,
at its root, to be amazed is to be dazed or bewildered; now
that gives the word more dimension. In today's gospel, Jesus
has read from the prophet Isaiah the passage that talks about
God anointing one to bring glad tidings to the poor, liberty
to captives, healing to the blind and deaf, and freedom for
the oppressed. Anyone assigned to read at the synagogue
would have proclaimed the same words. It is when Jesus
adds, "Today this Scripture passage is fulfilled in your hearing" that people are filled with surprise or are bewildered.
The real question is not whether Jesus should have added
his own commentary, but whether those who are amazed
will move from wonder to belief, or from being dazed to
being disciples.

So many things can cause us to be amazed: a compelling
story of heroism, witnessing the forces of nature, the beauty
of a symphony, the birth of a child. Such awe is essential to
shaping us as humans. I would venture to say further that

without wonder in our lives, we might never be drawn into and beyond the material world to discover God. In the Bible, amazement can lead to insight or discovery. Discovery has the power to move us from wonder to devotion. But devotion without discipleship will leave us without a share in the mission of Jesus.

Meditation: It is easy enough to become an observer in our faith life, as if visiting a museum or an art gallery. We love and admire what we're seeing and could spend all day just wandering the halls in admiration. But faith is not a gallery of wonderful ideas or admirable individuals. Jesus invites us to interact with what we see and hear, and to enter into a relationship with him. Then we become more than consumers; we become the converted. We learn to walk as Jesus did, extending his touch and his truth into the world. We become disciples.

Prayer: Jesus, your words and deeds continue to amaze us when we stop long enough to truly hear and see. Give us the curiosity to wonder at your presence in our world, and the commitment to stand and walk with you in our daily lives.

Take Notice

Readings: 1 John 5:5-13; Luke 5:12-16

Scripture:
"Lord, if you wish, you can make me clean." (Luke 5:12)

Reflection: I've never forgotten the face of a man who stopped me and a friend as we were heading out to a special dinner we had planned at a French restaurant. It was bitterly cold and we were making our way under scaffolding covered in ice next to a church being renovated. The man in front of us was having trouble navigating his way on the slick sidewalk, and when we reached him, he turned and simply said, "I'm hungry." His face was weathered and the tears he had been shedding formed ice down his cheeks. Our plans changed immediately. A nearby chicken house seated us in the very back and begrudgingly served us our food. He was homeless, estranged from what was left of his family in another province, and had not eaten since arriving by bus several days before our encounter. With no connections in the city, he was desperate, and we were given the opportunity to help him find shelter and assistance.

What strikes me most about people who are homeless or ill is that in addition to practical help, they need a sense of belonging. The man in today's gospel account is "full of leprosy" and as a result would have been ostracized from his community. Imagine the immense need that would have led him to approach Jesus, fall to the ground at Jesus' feet, and plead to be made clean. The healing he received not only cured his sores and restored his skin, but surely also brought him from the edges of society to the center.

Meditation: Spirituality could be described as taking notice, of allowing enough room in our plans and in our hearts to notice who Jesus is placing right in front of us. The man whose leprosy kept him separated from others noticed Jesus, and in the midst of being surrounded by people and moving from town to town, Jesus noticed him. Jesus took note of the man's condition, of his need, of his courage, and then Jesus took that sacred pause to acknowledge him and heal him. How has the Lord taken notice of you? And who is waiting for you to notice them?

Prayer: Jesus, you appear in our lives in the faces of those we meet and in the expressed needs that we are challenged to address. Gift us with awareness, and fill us with compassion. Interrupt our plans so that we will learn to take notice of your people.

Allow Jesus to Increase

Readings: 1 John 5:14-21; John 3:22-30

Scripture:
"He must increase; I must decrease." (John 3:30)

Reflection: A man and woman I know used their creativity and hard work to create some innovative products, leading their company to be quite successful over time. The couple decided to sell their company to another individual who could continue the innovations. I was stunned to discover much later that they shared their profits with all of their employees, hand-delivering checks to each person and thanking them for their particular gifts and talents. Ann and Tim (because they would be embarrassed, I have changed their names) knew with certainty that they could not have succeeded on their own. Their success was not to their credit but to the credit of the team, and by the grace of God. They were willing to decrease so that others would increase, and not just financially.

Actually, John the Baptist's words, "He must increase; I must decrease," could apply to so many characters in the New Testament. Mary of Magdala gave witness to the resurrection and then is rarely heard from again. While women's roles were quite limited at the time of Jesus, I have a feeling she would also understand it was about Jesus, not about her.

Barnabas and Peter, so prominent in the first half of Acts, faded a bit as Paul emerged. Paul credited Apollos with having planted the seeds of faith that he watered, and acknowledged that God causes the growth, not him (1 Cor 3). Ego is no match for God's grace, and all of us who minister in the name of Jesus know that it is Christ who takes center stage.

Meditation: It is only natural to be proud of accomplishments and to know that the investments we have made with our life's energies are bearing fruit. It can be deeply satisfying to know that our talents are being put to good use. The danger, however, is when ego becomes the driving force in our work and ministries. Jesus must increase, and I must decrease.

Prayer: You, O Lord, are generous in sharing the work of your kingdom with us. Give us the same generosity in our work. When we collaborate with others, be the center of our efforts. Help us to know when to step out of the light to let others shine with your radiance.

Be Expectant

Readings: Isa 40:1-5, 9-11; Titus 2:11-14; 3:4-7; Luke 3:15-16, 21-22

Scripture:
The people were filled with expectation. . . . (Luke 3:15)

Reflection: Charles Dickens famously begins his novel *A Tale of Two Cities* with this line: "It was the best of times, it was the worst of times, it was the age of wisdom, it was the age of foolishness, it was the epoch of belief, it was the epoch of incredulity. . . ." His novel, of course, was a way of commenting on the atmosphere in England and in France at the time of the French Revolution of the eighteenth century. The rich got richer and the poor were left behind. Law and order were enforced based on appearances and social connections rather than justice. Violence and unrest was the order of the day. Perhaps these cultural realities are not so far removed from any period in history, including the time of Jesus and John the Baptist.

The natural response to foreign occupiers (the Romans, for example) and corruption (in civic and religious leadership) might be apprehension, hopelessness, or even revolt. But our gospel today tells us the people are filled with expectation. They have been listening to John the Baptist rail against sin and injustice, they came to be baptized, and they wonder if he is the Messiah they have been awaiting.

John's preaching turned the people inward in repentance and then outward toward a future that was brimming with possibility. They would begin to see the best of times in the midst of the worst, find wisdom in what others saw as foolish, and be grounded in faith rather than mired in doubt.

Meditation: The feast of the Baptism of the Lord is a fitting way to close the Christmas season. The child from our manger scenes has grown up and become a man. Whatever hopes the shepherds and the magi felt that long-ago Christmas night are now being put to the test as Jesus launches his public ministry. Expectation was the order of the day as we began Advent, and expectation is the ending note of the Christmas season. The question now is how we will sound the notes of hope and expectation in our lives as disciples.

Prayer: Lord Jesus, your coming into our world is pure gift. Make us worthy ambassadors of your name and your kingdom, providing a well of expectant hope for a weary world.

References

November 29: Monday of the First Week of Advent
Second Vatican Council, Pastoral Constitution on the Church in the Modern World (*Gaudium et Spes*) 80, in Austin Flannery, ed., *Vatican Council II: Constitutions, Decrees, Declarations; The Basic Sixteen Documents* (Collegeville, MN: Liturgical Press, 2014).

December 13: Saint Lucy, Virgin and Martyr
Saint Pope John Paul II, *Redemptoris Missio* 2 (on the permanent validity of the church's missionary mandate), 1990, http://www.vatican.va/content/john-paul-ii/en/encyclicals/documents/hf_jp-ii_enc_07121990_redemptoris-missio.html.

December 17: Friday of the Third Week of Advent
For more information about restorative justice, see *Redemption and Restoration: A Catholic Perspective on Restorative Justice* (Collegeville, MN: Liturgical Press, 2017).

December 24:
Friday of the Fourth Week of Advent (Christmas Eve)
CBS Evening News, December 12, 2013, https://www.youtube.com/watch?v=uptsIngNxCY.
Mohandes K. Gandhi, *All Men Are Brothers: Autobiographical Reflections* (New York: Bloomsbury, 2013; first published by UNESCO, 1958), 182.

December 29:
Fifth Day within the Octave of the Nativity of the Lord
For more information about the ministry known as Settled Souls,
see https://www.lumenchristiaward.org/settled-souls.

December 31:
Seventh Day within the Octave of the Nativity of the Lord
For lyrics to Tevye's song, see https://www.allmusicals.com
/lyrics/fiddlerontheroof/tolife.htm.

January 9: The Baptism of the Lord
Charles Dickens, *A Tale of Two Cities* (London: Global Classics,
2017 edition of 1859 printing), 9.